# Reflections.

Realising the power of
Appreciative Inquiry:
an Appreciative Journal
and practical resource book

WORDSCAPES

# Reflections.

## Realising the power of Appreciative Inquiry: an Appreciative Journal and practical resource book

Written by Suzanne Quinney and Tim Slack
Design and production: Rhian Askins
Editors: Andrew Beattie and Fiona Shaw
Proofreading by Lucy Chesters

Printed and bound in the UK by Resolution Print Management

ISBN: 978-0-9955594-8-6

First published in November 2017 by Wordscapes Ltd.
The Mezzanine, Northern Lights Building, 5 Mann Street
Liverpool L8 5AF
www.wordscape.org.uk

# Contents

# Foreword

We have known and worked with Tim and Suzanne for at least the past ten years and it has been a delight for us to know them as friends and colleagues. Previous AI publications by Appreciating People have always been creative, practical and supportive. We believe you will find *Reflections* to be the same.

We know that to take time to reflect on life actions leads to new learnings and strengthening the things we think we do well.

We invite you to take to heart the 21-day appreciative journal programme offered in *Reflections*. We think it will, in fact, strengthen your practice of Appreciative Inquiry. And, more importantly will strengthen your 'appreciative eye' and open you to have a broader and deeper sense of gratitude.

The insights to the AI principles and the simple practical AI activities included here we know will support you in your AI journey.

Thanks to Appreciating People for adding this resource to the Appreciative Inquiry Community.

Jane Magruder Watkins
Ralph Kelly

# Welcome and introduction

*"Cultivating an appreciative voice not only strengthens you and expands your world, it also strengthens others and expands their worlds"* Robyn Stratton-Berkessel, 2017

This book is designed for Appreciative Inquiry (AI) practitioners at the start of your AI journey. It provides a short appreciative journal to help you develop your 'appreciative muscle', information on the AI principles, and tools and activities to support your interventions and help you reflect on your practice.

In the last three years we have delivered over 50 short AI courses for a wide range of organisations and community groups, focusing on practical applications of AI, encouraging people to build their 'appreciative muscle' and to 'be AI' in work and home life. Shifting our tendency to be drawn to a strength-based positive focus rather than a negative one takes practice. This is called developing 'an appreciative mindset'.

Our existing appreciative journals *Food for Thought* and *How to be More Awesome* have helped people to move to this appreciative mindset. Recent experience indicates that a bespoke 21-day programme, including Seven Day Acts of Gratitude, would be a compact and effective approach.

This publication intends to provide an accessible journaling experience for those people who have felt daunted by long term journaling and haven't yet had the opportunity to experience its benefits. It also addresses the oft-expressed concern of 'I really like this way of working, but how do I start? I need something practical and accessible.' We want to provide examples of activities to help people get started with AI.

*Reflections* has been two years in gestation, with much testing and reflection. We have been encouraged by AI practitioners such as Dr Lindsey Godwin, Matt Moehle, Jackie Kelm, Robyn Stratton-Berkessel, Cati Paya, Anita Sheehan, Francesca Olivia, and our partners.

Special thanks to our sponsors the West Midlands Patient Safety Collaborative, which is part of the West Midlands Academic Health Science Network (WMAHSN); the David L. Cooperrider Global Center for AI; and Appreciating Church. Information about the sponsors can be found on page 100.

Our appreciative journaling approach and the section on the principles have been significantly influenced by, and draws from Jackie Kelm's great work – *Appreciative Living* (see page 50).

We hope you will find *Reflections* a valuable resource in your AI practitioner journey, wherever this life-giving and generative process takes you. Please let us know your thoughts – we love hearing about your progress.

Tim Slack and Suzanne Quinney, Appreciating People
**www.appreciatingpeople.co.uk  @AppreciatingP**

## Further AI information

AI reading lists are found throughout Appreciating People publications – you'll find them at **www.aiessentials.co.uk**

**www.appreciatingpeople.co.uk** also has a range of useful blogs on examples of AI practice.

# Part one:
# Why journal?

# How to use *Reflections* and make the most of appreciative journaling

We suggest that you begin this journey by journaling. Our experience, and positive psychology research, indicates that recording three good things for 21 days has a profound positive effect on your wellbeing and bolsters your appreciative mindset. Undertaking and recording acts of gratitude equally fosters positivity and appreciation. We have concentrated on a 21-day programme, plus seven gratitude days (page 12).

If you're interested in continuing your journaling, look at *Food for Thought* or *How to be More Awesome*, which are available from **www.aiessentials.co.uk.**

After reading the Purcell article below and also watching Shawn Achor's TED talk, *The Happiness Advantage*, we hope that you feel intrigued enough to try out journaling for yourself. When you decide to start the journaling process, consider the best time for you to do it. It could be last thing at night or first thing in the morning, reflecting on the previous day. Use images and drawings as well as writing down thoughts and reflections. At the end you'll find a couple of exercises to help you reflect on and learn from your journaling.

# Why is journaling important?

*"People travel to wonder at the height of the mountains, at the huge waves of the seas, and yet they pass by themselves without wondering."* St. Augustine

The word 'journaling' comes from the word 'journey'. Writing and using a journal is a personal endeavour and a confidential process. Sharing information about the experience (rather than the content) is a great educational and learning opportunity. Many of the exercises and tasks can be shared and used to chart people's progress. The important thing is that this needs be part of a personal decision, and you can ask for support/encouragement on the journey from a friend or mentor. *

Journaling is an ancient tradition. Throughout history, people have kept journals and diaries, and these have made a rich contribution to our understanding of history. There is increasing research to support the idea that journaling has a positive effect on personal wellbeing and provides a range of unexpected benefits.

The act of writing accesses the left brain, which is analytical and rational. While your left brain is occupied, your right brain is free to create, be intuitive and feel. Recording things in your journal can help remove mental blocks. It allows you to use all your brain power and strengths to better understand yourself, others and the world around you. Journaling has a number of benefits:

1. It helps you to clarify your thoughts – taking a few moments to write down ideas can help you sort out the jumble of thoughts inside your brain.

2. It helps you to know yourself better – observing and writing regularly helps you get to know what makes you feel happy and confident, appreciate yourself, connect with your strengths, provide a clear view on situations and actions you're thinking of taking, and people you may have to deal with, all of which are important for your emotional wellbeing.

3. Journaling helps to reduce stress – writing about things that upset and challenge you helps to release these feelings, so you'll feel calmer and better able to cope.

4. It helps solve problems more effectively – typically we solve problems via a left brain analytical perspective, but sometimes the problem can only be solved by engaging right-brained creativity and intuition. Writing and recording thoughts (including drawing and sketching them) unlocks those abilities, providing the opportunity for unexpected solutions to arise.

5. It also helps you to resolve disagreements with others. Writing and recording about misunderstandings, concerns and issues can help you avoid stewing. It will help you to understand different views and contribute to a resolution.

6. Journaling allows you to track patterns, trends, improvements, and personal development over a period of time.

* Purcell, M. (2006): *The Health Benefits of Journaling in Psych Central.* Retrieved on June 25, 2014, from **http://psychcentral.com/lib/the-health-benefits-of-journaling/000721**

Appreciative journaling adds another dimension to the journaling experience. It's about actively seeking the good side of a situation and seeing how we can expand on that. We're not asking you to ignore or whitewash difficult situations or experiences – but rather than wasting energy on things which increase your negative emotions, search out and focus on positive ones.

# What we put our attention on grows in our minds

Ruminating is the name we give to focusing on negative thoughts – it's like a record that's stuck and keeps repeating the same lines. Research has shown that rumination is associated with a variety of negative consequences; appreciative journaling is a very helpful alternative. Feel free to record things that are bothering you – it can be a good way to stop the rumination cycle. Byron Katie sums it up when she says: "All war belongs on paper."

# The importance of gratitude and the 'happiness advantage'

We tend to think 'I'll be happy when I get a promotion and when I feel my work is recognised', or 'I'll be happy when I am fit enough or thin enough'. Whenever we reach a goal our happiness level doesn't really rise – we just set ourselves another goal we have to reach. Shawn Achor writes very clearly about the need to turn our way of thinking on its head – be happy first, and let success follow.

If we can be happy in the moment rather than deferring it until we are 'successful', then the brain experiences a happiness advantage. Your brain performs better – intelligence rises, your creativity and energy rises. Dopamine makes you happier and turns on the learning centres in your brain; the brain becomes 31% more effective – 37% better at sales; doctors are 19% better at correctly diagnosing patients. In just two minutes a day, for 21 days in a row, your brain can be rewired to work more optimistically and more successfully – just by writing down three new things each day that you appreciate.

Journaling about one positive experience over the past 24 hours allows your brain to relive it and you receive the benefits. Exercise teaches your brain that your behaviour matters. Meditation and mindfulness help us undo the stress of multi-tasking. Sending one text or Facebook message to a friend stating something you appreciate about them, or strength of theirs that you like, can create ripples of positivity.

(Comments taken from *The Happiness Advantage: The seven principles of positive psychology that fuel success and performance at work* and *The happy secret to better work* - Shawn Achor's TED talk: **www.ted.com/talks/lang/en/ shawn_achor_the_happy_secret_to_better_work.html**.)

**Negativity bias** explains how things of a negative nature – like unpleasant thoughts, social interactions or traumatic events – have a greater effect on our psychological state and behaviour than neutral or positive things. This means that we need to give more attention to the positive in order for our brain to retain positive information well. Alison Ledgerwood has an excellent TED talk on the subject, called *Getting stuck in the negatives (and how to get unstuck)*.

*"The negative screams at you but the positive only whispers"* Barbara Frederickson

Notice in your journal when you are falling into the trap of negativity bias, and notice what your positivity ratio is – both in your dialogue with yourself and with others. See if you can keep it at 3:1 or more – three positive statements to one negative.

# Appreciative journaling: an example

We're grateful for these thoughts and ideas from Nick Moore, who has maintained a journal for many years now.

I write down three things every day as a minimum, as per Jackie Kelm's stuff, although I can't remember the last time I only had three. If there were only three it's important not to put pressure on yourself – it's just that usually there really is more than that. I tend to do it every night, but fit it in when it works for you.

I also use the Seligman (from *Flourish* by Martin Seligman) questions – he recommends writing three things too. Sometimes I just write the three things because I guess they stand for themselves. Depending on how late at night it is, and how much energy I have, it's helpful to answer one of the following questions for each thing. Just choose whichever you like:

Why did this go well?

Why did this good thing happen?

What does this mean to me?

How can I have more of this good thing in the future?

I also do the Jackie Kelm thing – note one thing, no matter how small, to increase my joy. It can be a small or a large thing – sometimes there's more than one, and sometimes several of varying importance.

Once a week I make notes on my ideal life, or – more usually for me – I work through Jackie's appreciative living cards (www.appreciativeliving.com). I'm not too planned about this and sometimes I'll do two or three fairly close together.

What I tend to do is write the quote and the question in my journal a few days before I'm likely to answer it. That way I've read the question, and find it helps my thinking when the time comes to write up my answer.

I find the cards very helpful because they ask me more varied questions from different angles – I find that reflective process very important and moving.

For the things that went well, there are all sorts of things that go in here and the great thing is that I'd never reflect on some of them, without this process.

So, I have things that went well at work sessions, meetings, conversations, my day's run; but also appreciation of others – seeing people grow and develop and meeting new people. There are beautiful mornings, rainbows seen out of the office window, nice things my wife Lesley does for me, meetings with family and old friends, nice emails and phone calls, programmes on the radio and listening to good bits of music – stuff I know and new to me stuff – appreciation of books, articles, TV programmes, company I have enjoyed, nice journeys. And lots of other things besides...

Lots of these are nice small things, but it's good to pay respect to them as well as the big stuff. The small stuff is very important. Even people dying, whom I like, can be acknowledged because I was blessed by their lives. So when the former Brazilian footballer Socrates died in December 2011, but whose football I enjoyed a lot in the '80s, it was great seeing some of his wonderful goals replayed.

Nick Moore, www.MooreInsight.co.uk
(*MooreInsight is a co-creator of the Collaborative Inquiry workbook.*)

*"Appreciation is a wonderful thing. It makes what is excellent in others belong to us as well."*
Voltaire

# Part two:
# The journal

# 21 days of journaling; seven days of gratitude and reflecting on your journaling experience

For the next 21 days, write down or doodle three good things that happen to you on each day. They can be small – *I helped a colleague answer a query; a friend appreciated something I did; I saw a beautiful sunset.*

Against each positive event, write:

· Why did this good thing happen?

· What does it mean to me?

· How can I have more of it?

# Journal, day 1 🖉

*Three good things...*

*"Gratitude is the open door to the power, the wisdom the creativity of the universe. You open the door through gratitude."*
Deepak Chopra

12

# Journal, day 2 🖉

*Three good things...*

*"I don't mind being wrong, and I don't mind changing my mind."*
Martin Seligman

# Journal, day 3 🖉
## *Three good things...*

*"Act as if you what you do makes a difference — it does."*

William James

# Journal, day 4 ✏

*Three good things...*

# Journal, day 5 ✏️

## *Three good things...*

*"We are what we repeatedly do. Excellence, then, is not an act, but a habit."*

Aristotle

# Journal, day 6 ✏️

*Three good things...*

# Journal, day 7 ✎

*Three good things...*

*"True wisdom
comes to each
of us when we
realise how little
we understand
about life,
ourselves, and
the world
around us."*

Socrates

# Journal, day 8 🖉

## *Three good things...*

*"There are only two ways to live your life. One is as though nothing is a miracle. The other is as though everything is a miracle."*
Albert Einstein

# Journal, day 9 🖉

*Three good things...*

*"The significance is hiding in the insignificant — appreciate everything"*

Eckhart Tolle

# Journal, day 10 🖉

## *Three good things...*

*"Imagination is more important than knowledge."*
Albert Einstein

# Journal, day 11 🖉

*Three good things...*

*"Turn your face towards the sun and the
shadows will fall behind you."*
Maori proverb

# Journal, day 12 ✎

*Three good things...*

*"Habits are at first cobwebs, then cables."*
Spanish proverb

# Journal, day 13 🖉

*Three good things...*

*"Strength shows not only in the ability to persist but the opportunity to start over."*
F. Scott Fitzgerald

# Journal, day 14

*Three good things...*

*"If we can create our world
view, we can recreate it too by
taking a different perspective and
reframing our situation."*
Ken Robinson

# Journal, day 15 🖉

*Three good things...*

*"If opportunity did not knock, build a door."*
Milton Berle

# Journal, day 16 ✏

*Three good things...*

*"Wisdom begins in wonder."*
Socrates

# Journal, day 17 ✏️

*Three good things...*

# Journal, day 18 ✎

*Three good things...*

*"If you're not failing every now and again, it's a sign you're not doing anything very innovative."*
Woody Allen

# Journal, day 19 ✎

*Three good things...*

*"Forget your perfect offering, there is
a crack in everything. That's how the
light gets in."*
Leonard Cohen

# Journal, day 20 ✏️

*Three good things...*

# Journal, day 21 🖉

*Three good things...*

> *"Failures, repeated failures, are finger posts on the road to achievement. One fails forward toward success."*
>
> C. S. Lewis

# Journaling reflections

*"Happiness can be found even in the darkest times if only ones remembers to turn on the light."*
Albus Dumbledore in Harry Potter and the Prisoner of Azkaban

# The seven day Acts of Gratitude activity

Take a few moments to think of a colleague or friend whom you'd like to thank for something they've done. Then think about an action that they would appreciate. It could be making them a card, sending a thank you email, making a small gift, or just telling them verbally.

Keep a note of what you did and anything that emerged from it. Acts of gratitude help your mental health and wellbeing. You can find out more about the importance of gratitude by researching on the internet.

Thanks to positive psychology research and associated work, it's clear that gratitude has a number of well-researched benefits. It reduces stress and anxiety, and supports our optimism, health and wellbeing, and our social relations – to build new ones and make current ones better. Acts of gratitude can be used to apologise, make amends or help solve other problems people may face. Simply being grateful for being alive is a great way to meet the day.

Research in 2015 on patients with heart failure reported that those who completed gratitude journals showed reduced inflammation, improved sleep and better moods after only eight weeks. A study by McCraty and colleagues (1998), taught 45 adults to 'cultivate appreciation and other **positive emotions**'. The results showed a mean 23% reduction in the stress hormone cortisol after the intervention period.

Gratitude helps us be more effective at work, helps us network, builds our resilience and increases decision making capacities; it makes our workplaces a more friendly and enjoyable place to be. In sport, gratitude exercises have been used to help prepare athletes for a productive practice and foster cohesion within a team.

# Gratitude, day 1

*"Children are happy because they don't have a file in their minds called 'All the Things That Could Go Wrong'."*
Marianne Williamson

# Gratitude, day 2

*"I would maintain that thanks are the highest form of thought; and that gratitude is happiness doubled by wonder."*

G.K. Chesterton

# Gratitude, day 3

*"At times, our own light goes out and is rekindled by a spark from another person. Each of us has cause to think with deep gratitude of those who have lighted the flame within us."*

Albert Schweitzer

# Gratitude, day 4

*"Piglet noticed
that even
though he had
a Very Small
Heart, it could
hold a rather
large amount of
Gratitude."*
A.A. Milne

# Gratitude, day 5

# Gratitude, day 6

*"Gratitude is the healthiest of all human emotions. The more you express gratitude for what you have, the more likely you will have even more to express gratitude for."*

Zig Ziglar

# Gratitude, day 7

"*We can always choose to perceive things differently. We can focus on what's wrong in our life, or we can focus on what's right.*"
Marianne Williamson

# After your seven days of gratitude, consider these questions:

· How did the acts of gratitude make you feel?

· What did you notice in yourself?

· What was the impact on the recipients? Did it affect the relationships?

# Further reflection on your journaling experience

This short appreciative conversation is designed to share your use of, and reflection on, your appreciative journal. It is about your learning journey. Please note that you don't need to share any personal information that you put in your journal, but we suggest that someone interviews you and the responses are recorded in the journal.

· Share an example of one of your best experiences of using the journal...

· What have you enjoyed most about it?

· What changes have you noticed about yourself, your thinking, and your attitudes whilst using the journal?

· Which examples of learning or noticing arising from the appreciative journal experience do you want to continue to use and practice?

· What did you notice happened when you did the act of gratitude activity – in yourself and the people you engaged with?

*"The moment one gives close attention to anything, even a blade of grass, it becomes a mysterious, awesome, indescribably magnificent world in itself."*

Henry Miller

# The Seven Cs and journaling

The *My Home Life* leadership support programme uses *Caring Conversations*, a flexible practice framework to support practitioners to facilitate the development of generative, appreciative and relational capacities in care settings. Within the framework there are questions that can be used in any settings; we've made some suggestions as to how it might support journaling. The Seven Cs are:

1. **Connecting** emotionally – notice when you have made an emotional connection with other people and the effect it had on your day.

2. **Considering** other perspectives – deepen how you view daily interactions. Journal what you've noticed about others' perspectives and how this information has supported your interactions with them.

3. **Curiosity** – a benevolent curiosity is a key component of AI. Bring your sense of wonder and curiosity into your journaling.

4. **Collaborating** – notice the moments when you have collaborated with other people in an appreciative way.

5. **Compromising** – when have you made a compromise which has led to a better outcome for all concerned?

6. **Courageous** – be brave and bold in your positive journaling. It's a place to practice new attitudes and ways of thinking before you exercise them in the world.

7. **Celebrating** – celebrate when you've had an appreciative day – of yourself or of others. Celebrate when you've used your strengths or brought other people's strengths to light. Celebrate when you have noticed your negative bias and not gone down that route.

Thanks to Belinda Dewar and colleagues in *My Home Life* for creating this and allowing us to adapt it. You'll find more at **myhomelife.uws.ac.uk/scotland/resources** including case studies, videos, articles, posters and a wealth of information and resources on using AI.

# Report your excellence

You might find completing an excellence report on yourself useful, if unusual.

Our involvement in the Learning from Excellence programme (described on page 62) has been one of our key inspirations to produce this journal. So, as part of your journal we would also like to encourage you to notice everyday excellence in the notes you make and stories that you capture – your own and other peoples'. It is often a challenge for us to name our strengths and reflect on the things that we do well – naming our own excellence raises the bar for us one notch higher – try it!

*"Whatever your discipline, become a student of excellence in all things. Take every opportunity to observe people who manifest the qualities of mastery. These models of excellence will inspire you and guide you toward the fulfilment of your highest potential."*

Michael Gelb and Tony Buzan

# Part three: Philosophy and principles

## Background to the philosophy and principles, and a powerful story about appreciation and learning

We've included a basic reminder of what AI is and an outline of its tools. One of the challenges for the AI practitioner is getting your head around the principles. Drawing deeply and quoting extensively from Jackie Kelm's *Appreciative Living* we have provided extra information on these principles. Thank you Jackie for your support and inspiration! Please see *Appreciative Living* for sources and references. At the beginning of part four (page 72) there are a couple of exercises to help you deepen your understanding of the AI principles.

# Appreciative Inquiry – philosophy, and practice

Appreciative Inquiry (AI) is an organisational and community development philosophy and approach which focuses and builds on 'what works' and the existing strengths and assets.

The term 'appreciative' comes from the idea that when something increases in value it 'appreciates'. 'Inquiry' describes the process of seeking to understand through questions and the value of paying attention to the things that, if increased, would add value and make a difference.

AI is the cousin of positive psychology and part of the growing movement to focus on and build from the strengths and assets of people and groups. By working from this positive focus, as opposed to focusing on what's not working, people become more resilient and creative. They develop and deliver success and achieve realistic solutions to problems.

First developed by David Cooperrider in the late 1980s at Case Western University in the USA, AI is now used all over the world by large and small organisations, communities, and in personal development programmes. At the heart of the approach are questions and conversations that are interesting, informative and help you learn about yourself and the people and groups around you.

*"AI is a process for engaging people in building the kinds of organisations and a world they want to live in. Working from people's strengths and positive experiences, AI co-creates a future based on collaboration and dialogue."* David Cooperrider

There are three useful tools within AI: the paired conversation (sometimes called a protocol), which consists of a number of questions to deeply explore a topic (examples in part four, on page 74). The second is the 5D process for projects (you'll find a drawing on the next page), and for large scale events (called AI summits); and third is SOAR™ (strengths, opportunities, aspirations and resources/results) – the AI alternative to a SWOT analysis (see page 91).

It's important to remember that AI is more than positive thinking, it is about how we both individually and collectively create change. It's not about ignoring problems, but looking at them differently. Alongside a model for organisational and community development, AI has contributed to different approaches in mentoring, coaching, leadership, team building, counselling and international development. It is the key underpinning methodology to all Appreciating People's journals. More information on Appreciative Inquiry and its application can be found at **www.appreciatingpeople.co.uk.**

# The 5Ds cycle

**Definition**
'what is the inquiry?'
Choose an affirmative topic

**Destiny/ Delivery**
...creating
'what will be'
Innovation and improvisation

**Discovery**
...appreciating
'the best of what is'
Share stories

**Design**
...determining
'what should be'
Design prototypes – reconceive and redesign structures and processes

**Dream**
...imagining
'what could be'
Conversations and images of possibility and potential

Positive Core

# SOAR™

What are our resources?
What are the measurable results?

What do we aspire to be?

What do we
to get ther
How will we
we've got th

What are the opportunities?

What are our greatest strengths and assets?

What is our collective intention?
What is our desired future?

What are the best things out there for us?
What can we do differently?

What works here?
What do we do well?

S O A R™

# The principles behind AI

The AI principles are at the heart of Appreciative Inquiry and repay bountifully any time taken to study them. Noticing their occurrence and impact in your AI practitioner journal is a good way to build this awareness. Jackie Kelm provides an illuminative and practical description of the AI principles in her book *Appreciative Living*. With her permission the following section is drawn extensively from this brilliant resource. Her work is extensively referenced which space has not permitted us to do – so please refer to *Appreciative Living* for details. We recommend it for further reading on any of the principles.

# The Constructionist Principle

*"We are in continuous conversation with each other and with ourselves. Through conversation we form and reform our life experiences and events; we create and recreate our meanings and understandings; and we construct and reconstruct our realities and our selves. Some conversations enhance possibility; others diminish it."* Harlene Anderson

Reality is co-created in communication through words and dialogues with others and with ourselves. Multiple interpretations of what is real co-exist – we're constantly co-creating our reality with every conversation and social interaction. We create stories to make sense of things, but our stories are not the truth, just one perspective and interpretation – **we are never neutral observers.**

The language we use and the conversations we take part in all contribute to how we construct our world and the world of those we talk to. Other people's language and images/metaphors in conversations reveal elements of their construction. Each person's reality is subjective. There is no right or wrong reality – just a difference of interpretation.

This can often be seen in family members having very different recollections of shared events – for example two young siblings being told to wait in the garden while the house is being prepared for a party – one remembers the excitement of waiting to come in, while the other remembers the feeling of being shut out and excluded.

Kenneth and Mary Gergen talk about 'local truth,' an agreement about what is true within a community of people. The truths that are created within communities have meaning and value within those communities, but not necessarily beyond, and others outside the community may not see it the same way. How we tell our story or our organisation's story influences the way in which we change and the direction of change.

*"Our own life is the instrument with which we experiment with truth."* Thich Nhat Hanh

# The Simultaneity Principle

## Change begins the moment we question

*"All questions are leading questions."* Michael Hoyt

Rather than assuming that we can know reality in any definitive and unquestioning way, we can explore it as something which is changing. The moment we inquire, or ask a question, we initiate a reaction at many different levels of our consciousness. The moment you ask a question, you've started a narrative journey. The language, tone and intention of the question determine the direction of the conversation. So, when you create questions, consider what you're really seeking to learn more about. How can you encourage the respondent to reflect on what is valuable and important? Warren Berger's book title sums it up, *A More Beautiful Question: The Power of Inquiry to Spark Breakthrough Ideas*. To get the best answers, we have to ask the best possible question.

Cooperrider and Whitney explain: It is not so much 'Is my question leading to right or wrong answers?' But rather 'What impact is my question having on our lives together? Is it helping to generate conversations about the good, the better, the possible? Is it strengthening our relationships?'

Appreciative conversations on their own have a transformative power.

*"Evidence from a steel mill trying to improve safety performance underscores how organisations go in the direction of what they ask the most questions about... Conversations dramatically shape individual and collective behaviour. The conversations were designed and facilitated to prepare for an AI summit; however the safety improved soon after the conversations started, and including nearly all voices in the system led to generative connections and significant behaviour changes."*

Ron Fry in *AI Practitioner* (May 2012)

Jackie Kelm offers a great example of the power of a 'full scale positive question', prefaced by an evocative poem by Mary Jean Iron:

*"Normal day, let me be aware of the treasure you are. Let me learn from you, love you, bless you before you depart. Let me not pass you by in quest of some rare and perfect tomorrow. Let me hold you while I may, for it may not always be so. One day I shall dig my nails into the earth, or raise my hands to the sky and want, more than all the world, your return."*

Each day offers the potential to see common life in miraculous new ways, and discover beauty in the ordinary. Singer and songwriter Joni Mitchell wrote, *"You don't know what you've got till it's gone."*

Examples of full scale positive questions:

**As you reflect on the gift of your 'average' day today, what is it that you appreciate?**

**If this were your last day here on earth and you could hold on to one aspect of it, what would it be and why?**

Psychology professor Mihaly Csikszentmihalyi suggests four steps in developing greater personal interest and curiosity in his book, *Flow*. They are:

1. Try to be surprised by something every day
2. Try to surprise at least one person every day
3. Write down each day what surprised you and how you surprised others
4. When something strikes a spark of interest, follow it

# The Anticipatory Principle

*"The future is not a result of choices among alternate paths offered by the present, but a place that is created… The future is not some place we are going to, but one we are creating. The paths are not to be found, but made, and the activity of making them changes both the maker and the destination."* John Schaar

We all live in a future state to some extent – we constantly look forward to what might be, prompting us to make decisions which influence our present condition and actions. Our future is a constructed reality, created by our present thinking and imagery. When we create positive, uplifting images of our future, we're more likely to make decisions and act to help us reach that desired future.

When we anticipate the worst, we fill ourselves with a sense of foreboding, fear and limitation; we hold back and don't embrace opportunity. The placebo effect – where it is demonstrated that our beliefs create the healing power – is a good demonstration of the power of the Anticipatory Principle.

Anticipatory influence can be seen powerfully in the vision process of AI, where people are encouraged to articulate a desired future in a creative way. We are then invited to **find small steps** that move in its direction. Margaret Wheatley proposes a metaphor for vision in *Leadership and the New Science*. She suggests we consider it as a field:

"In linear fashion we have most often conceived of vision as designing the future, creating a destination for the organisation. … It's a very strong Newtonian image, much like the old view of gravity. But what if we changed the science and looked at vision as a field… what would we do differently to use its formative influence? We would start by recognising that in creating a vision, we are creating a power, not a place; an influence, not a destination."

Debbie Ford explains how vision helps to inform our decisions: "In any given moment we are being guided by one of two maps: a vision map, which is a deliberate plan for our future; or a default map, which is made up of our past. Choices made from our default map – our repetitive, automatic programming – do not nourish our flames, nor do they move us closer to our dreams. And even though they may feel right to us, they do so simply because they are familiar."

*"Nobody exceeds beyond his or her wildest expectations, unless he or she begins with some wild expectations."* Ralph Charell

# The Poetic Principle

The Poetic Principle suggests that our past, present, or future can be endless sources of learning, inspiration, or interpretation – precisely like the endless interpretive possibilities in a good piece of poetry, book or film. We can find whatever we want in a person or situation: good and bad, right and wrong, beautiful and ugly.

What we choose to focus on creates our reality. The more attention we give to something, the more it expands as part of our experience. Mac Odell, a leading AI practitioner, puts it this way: "If you focus on problems, you find more problems. If you focus on successes, you find more successes."

AI assumes that each person and "living system has many untapped and rich and inspiring accounts of the positive." (Cooperrider and Whitney).

Focus is fateful – branches of quantum mechanics have been exploring the idea of the participative universe – how we create reality by what we pay attention to. This suggests that what we choose to notice in a situation becomes our reality and everything else falls by the proverbial wayside. Wheatley explains:

*".. the act of looking for certain information evokes the information we went looking for – and simultaneously eliminates our opportunity to observe other information...we create not only the present with our observations, but the past as well. It is the existence of observers who notice what is going on that imparts reality to everything."*

We have an unlimited number of ways we can create our current reality, but our decision to select one creates it and eliminates all others. In this sense, it is much more powerful to 'think to', rather than 'think from'. 'Thinking to' involves creating images and ideas about what we want, and 'thinking from' looks at how we can eliminate or fix something we don't want. 'Thinking to' is a creative act; 'thinking from' is destructive.

*"The task is not so much to see what no one yet has seen, but to think what nobody yet has thought about that which everybody sees."* Schopenhauer

We can have fun developing our appreciative eye and using this principle in reframing by, for example, turning 'pits' of unwanted things into 'peaks'. For example, in an open plan office the 'pit' might be that it's too noisy; this could be reframed into a 'peak' of 'it's a great buzz working here'. Reframing (page 84) and honouring of diversity of views are a basis for co-creativity and co-authoring a different story.

# The Positive Principle

*"This principle simply says, 'Whatever you focus on expands.' It's a powerful concept – it's why Edison often announced the invention of a device before he'd actually invented it. It's why Jim Carrey wrote himself a cheque for $10 million long before he ever made a movie. And you'll learn that there's no such thing as an idle thought and that all of us are way too cavalier and tolerant of our minds' wandering."* Pam Grout

The Positive Principle states, 'Momentum for change requires large amounts of positive affect and social bonding – things like hope, excitement, inspiration, caring, camaraderie, a sense of urgent purpose, and sheer joy in creating something meaningful together.' (Cooperrider and Whitney) Positive emotion creates energy and momentum for change, and provides important resources for short and long-term physical and mental health.

Barbara Frederickson's work is particularly informative for this principle. There are four main propositions in her *broaden-and-build* framework.

1. Positive emotions broaden the scope of attention and thought-action repertoires.

2. Positive emotions undo lingering negative emotions.

3. Positive emotions fuel psychological resiliency.

4. Positive emotions build psychological resilience and fuel upward spirals toward improved emotional wellbeing.

One of the most popular ways in AI to build positive emotion is to inquire into something called the **positive core**. On a personal level, the positive core contains our wisdom, knowledge, successful life strategies, positive attitudes, strengths, skills, aspirations, resources, and capabilities. Everyone and every situation has a positive core.

# The Five Emergent Principles

*"You cannot step twice into the same river, for waters are continuously flowing on."* Heraclitus

There are five additional principles proposed by AI practitioners. The Wholeness Principle, the Enactment Principle, and the Free Choice Principle were proposed in *The Power of Appreciative Inquiry* (Whitney and Trosten-Bloom). The Awareness Principle was recommended in *Dynamic Relationships: Unleashing the Power of Appreciative Inquiry in Daily Life* (Stavros and Torres). The Narrative Principle was suggested in *Appreciative Inquiry: A Positive Approach to Cooperative Capacity Building* (Barrett and Fry).

# The Wholeness Principle

*"The Wholeness Principle posits that the experience of wholeness brings out the best in people, relationships, communities, and organisations."* Whitney and Trosten-Bloom

The Wholeness Principle takes the Constructionist Principle one step further and suggests that we are not only influenced by those around us, but are actually part of a bigger collective or whole. There is a layer of complexity in the whole that is lost when its pieces are studied separately. Such fragmented thinking is pervasive in Western culture, and physicist David Bohm explains how we create the appearance of a fragmented world by thinking in a fragmentary way:

"In essence, the process of division is a way of thinking about things that is convenient and useful mainly in the domain of practical, technical and functional activities (e.g., to divide up an area of land into different fields where various crops are to be grown). However, when this mode of thought is applied more broadly to man's notion of himself and the whole world in which he lives (i.e., to his self-world view), then man... begins to see and experience himself and his world as actually constituted of separately existent fragments... and acts in such a way as to try to break himself and the world up, so that all seems to correspond to his way of thinking."

It is valuable to be aware of our fragmentary way of thinking and its effects. We are all part of creating the whole we experience, and survival depends on our ability to work together.

Consider a family dinner. The next time you sit down to eat with your family or a group of friends, try an experiment in perceiving the whole system. Mentally step back and admire the overall flow of conversation and activities and the role played by different parts. Consider the life experiences that have shaped and moulded this family to what it is today. Remember that whatever we focus on grows, and we can find whatever we want within this experience. Try to look for what you want more of, not less of. In what ways are you supporting positive shifts? What would happen if you spoke about the shifts you are observing?

Wholeness creates deeper understandings of the complexity of the system. Ideas for change emerge as we immerse ourselves within the larger community. We can simply shift our thinking to be more continuously aware of the larger web of relationships in which we exist, and awaken to our place within them.

# The Enactment Principle

*"Be the change you wish to see in the world."* Mahatma Gandhi

Whitney and Trosten-Bloom describe the Enactment Principle as, "Positive change comes about as images and visions of a more desired future are enacted in the present." Ralph Waldo Emerson said, "What you do speaks so loud that I cannot hear what you say." This principle is about reflecting on what we do and the degree to which it aligns with what we want, and that we can create our ideal future by making changes in the present that align with that future.

Changing our actions means walking the talk, even when you feel like you're wobbling on your feet. Enactment means practicing new behaviours and actions in the present before we have 'reached' our vision, big changes begin small – have a go and try it! We create change through our daily incremental conversations and actions that add up to larger changes over time. Appreciative journaling can play a big role here.

# The Free Choice Principle

*"In the truest sense, freedom cannot be bestowed; it must be achieved."* Franklin D. Roosevelt

Whitney and Trosten-Bloom say that the essence of the Free Choice Principle is that "free choice liberates power... People perform better and are more committed when they have freedom to choose how and what they contribute."

There are internal beliefs that impact our ability to choose freely. Consider a person who feels trapped in a job they dislike and continues to work there year after year because they truly believe it is the only reasonable way they can provide for their family. However, their own limiting thoughts about what is possible are playing a part, and surfacing limiting assumptions can be a powerful activity. In journaling, inquire into peak moments and experiences of personal freedom to create more of it.

*"An appreciative voice provides safety for others to speak their truths. It is invitational and watchful. An appreciative voice is unhurried and patient. It can reframe situations to be helpful and resourceful. It is flexible. The appreciative voice is inclusive. It acknowledges diversity and identifies opportunities to offer possibilities to hold the space for transformational shifts to emerge."*

Robyn Stratton-Berkessel

# The Awareness Principle

*"Let us not look back in anger, nor forward in fear, but around in awareness."* James Thurber

This principle suggests we become more aware of our automatic thinking habits and intentionally shifting them in ways that are consistent with the AI principles. A key part of this is becoming aware of underlying assumptions that influence how we feel and what we think. *The Work of Byron Katie* is an accessible way of surfacing and inquiring into stressful beliefs and assumptions and finding out who we are without our stories. Find out more at **thework.com/en**.

*"The Abracadabra Principle. Most people associate the word abracadabra with magicians pulling rabbits out of hats. It's actually an Aramaic term that translates into English as, 'I will create as I speak.' It's a powerful concept."*

Pam Grout, *E-Squared: Nine Do-It-Yourself Energy Experiments That Prove Your Thoughts Create Your Reality*

# The Narrative Principle

The Narrative Principle suggests that "stories weave a connectedness that bridges the past with the future." (Barrett and Fry) We create stories about ourselves and our lives that help us organise and make sense of things. We re-author our lives as we tell our stories.

Stories are transformative and extremely rich in meaning. They are imbued with images, metaphors, values, lessons, and a host of other things that reach deep inside us. Listening to the stories of others can be very powerful. Because they operate on emotional and metaphoric levels, stories move us before we 'know' why we are being moved. They reach us before we have a chance to put up our defences.

Stories from the past can convey values, norms, and traditions, which provide continuity and rationale in moving forward. Stories about the future contain powerful images which create that very future, as discussed in the Anticipatory Principle. They have transformative power by their very nature and profoundly influence our course. Better stories are those that bring more of what is desired and less of what is not. (see Adrian Plunkett's story opposite)

# Conclusion

You will notice that there is overlap between some of the principles – we liken them to a rope where, for the purpose of learning, we unpick the strands to study them more closely. But in daily life the rope functions as a single unit deriving its strength from the weaving together of the separate strands.

This quote from Viktor Frankl in *Man's Search for Meaning* illumines a profound application of the essence of these principles:

*"Everything can be taken from a man but one thing: the last of the human freedoms – to choose one's attitude in any given set of circumstances, to choose one's own way."*

# Learning from Excellence: a powerful story

As a reminder of the importance of story in Appreciative Inquiry, we use *A Tale of two SIRIs*. (A SIRI is a process used within the NHS when a serious error has been identified – it stands for Serious Incidents Requiring Investigation). The fable and the introduction below are written by Adrian Plunkett to give readers an idea of why he developed the *Learning from Excellence* programme.

"Our attempts to improve patient safety in the NHS have tended to focus on learning from error. Intuitively, this seems like a good idea: if we make a mistake, we would like to learn why it happened and how to stop it happening again. But errors only occur in a minority of clinical encounters, so our focus is narrow. We miss learning opportunities from the episodes when things have gone very well.

When excellence happens in healthcare, we tend to accept it gratefully and move on. Imagine if we could capture those episodes in order to understand how to repeat them. We might gain useful insights to improve quality of care, and improve staff morale through appreciation and recognition. This is the theory behind *Learning from Excellence* – a system for reporting and studying excellence in healthcare.

Our philosophy and a blog with resources is available on our website: **www.learningfromexcellence.com**. We have been capturing and studying excellence for over a year now, and encourage all healthcare professionals to do the same. The fable that follows describes a fictional NHS department."

*– Adrian Plunkett, consultant in Paediatric Intensive Care Medicine at Birmingham Children's Hospital*

**www.england.nhs.uk/signuptosafety/2015/11/26/adrian-plunkett/**

# A tale of two SIRIs

"Welcome everyone. Thanks for coming to this meeting. Shall we start with a quick round of introductions?" Julia hoped her cynicism didn't come across when she spoke. Having chaired many meetings, she was starting to doubt whether this process was effective. The purpose of the meeting was to investigate a medical error, to understand why it happened, and make recommendations to stop it happening again.

Julia had many years of clinical experience as a consultant anaesthetist, and a genuine interest in improving patient safety. So why was she starting to doubt the process? She had noticed that colleagues under investigation are almost always fearful; she saw them lose enthusiasm, become jaded, and become defensive in their work. Many of the recommendations from previous SIRIs were either not implemented, or were simply not effective; certain incidents seemed to keep occurring.

Let's keep this positive, and get it over with, she thought. James, the commissioner, started the introductions. He was the only member who Julia hadn't met before. It is a requirement of the SIRI process that a commissioner attends the meeting, but Julia found it uncomfortable discussing mistakes of the hospital in front of an external member. Thankfully, James spoke with a positive and empathetic tone during his introduction. Julia made a note to herself to tap his positivity if the meeting got a little too depressing.

Sandra and Gavin went next: both were consultant colleagues of Tim, who had made the error. Gavin had discovered it and filed the original incident report and, when reviewing the statements for this meeting, Julia couldn't help thinking that Gavin had been a little too efficient with the timing of his incident report. It might have been more helpful to let Tim report the incident himself.

Gavin's accompanying statement included several references to his own practice which didn't seem to serve any purpose other than to highlight his superiority. Sandra's statement, on the other hand, was brief and unhelpful, and looked like it had been written with minimal effort. Julia had worked with Sandra for many years and was well aware of Sandra's disdain for the patient safety investigation process. "The whole process is painful and pointless", Sandra had declared at a recent governance meeting. "Mistakes happen. We all drop the ball sometimes. We just need to be more careful, and get on with our jobs."

Tim introduced himself next. "I'm Tim. I'm the reason you're all here. I made the mistake, and … and, look… I'm sure it won't happen again." Tim was in his second year as a consultant anaesthetist. She remembered his statement had been brief but thoughtful, and tinged with regret. She had no doubt that he had learned from his mistake.

"I'm sure that's true, Tim," said Sandra. "Let's try to remember that this is not about apportioning blame. We are here today to try to understand why this happened, and to identify the root cause of the error, so we can prevent it happening again". As she spoke, she noticed James nodding in agreement. Gavin was smiling and Tim just looked at his papers on the desk.

And so the investigation started. Julia talked through the terms of reference for the investigation, then the event itself was discussed repeatedly in exquisite detail. All the 'evidence' came from the recollection of the staff members who were directly involved. Julia reflected that it was impossible to understand fully the context of the episode: was Tim tired that day; did he have a lot on his mind; were there a lot of distractions in theatre? None of this information was available.

The incident itself was a simple drug error: Tim had given a drug to which the patient was known to have a severe allergy. The patient had become unwell and required rapid intervention. While Tim was responding to the deterioration, Gavin had 'saved the day' – at least, that's what his statement had implied. Reading between the lines, it appeared that Tim had already picked up on the deterioration and was putting things right.

Nevertheless, a mistake had happened, and the patient had required a brief stay in intensive care. During the two-hour meeting Tim hardly spoke, other than to express regret and how he has learnt his lesson. By the end, the panel agreed that the root cause of the error was a failure of the whole team to carry out the patient safety checklist correctly – they had all missed the allergy when ticking the checklist items at the start of the case. Julia knew that this was an oversimplification, but it was the best they could do. The meeting finished with agreement over the recommendations to changes of practice to prevent a recurrence, re-emphasising existing guidelines and good practice.

After the meeting, Julia stayed behind and drafted an outline of the report before running to her afternoon theatre session on the plastic surgery list. As she took the last patient into recovery, Julia noticed a red band around the patient's wrist signifying severe allergy. She couldn't remember if she had been aware of the allergy, and found herself thinking about Tim, and how easy it can be to make a drug error.

Julia mulled over the day's events as she walked to the car park. As she reached her car door, she noticed she had parked next to Tim, who was sitting in the driver's seat, deep in thought. She knocked gently on his window and waved. He looked up, slightly embarrassed and let the window down. "Hi Julia. Thanks for being sympathetic today in the SIRI meeting". Tim looked sad and washed out. His spark had gone.

"It was a good meeting. I think we've come up with some good recommendations," she said, sounding a little unsure of herself.

"Yes, I'm sure you're right," said Tim. "The thing is, I'm still not sure the same error won't happen again to someone else. I keep thinking about that day and I think the problem is deeper than you think. There's a whole negative culture around the safety checklist. It's like no one really 'gets it' in that theatre."

Julia wondered why Tim hadn't mentioned this in the SIRI meeting. "Well, we did seem to agree that the root cause of the error was due to the failure of the checklist to highlight the allergy," she said.

"Yes, but I think it's deeper than that. The root cause analysis is a bit simplistic, don't you think?" Tim looked frustrated, slightly angry. "The world is more complex than that. There isn't a single root cause for every event. It's just not that simple."

Julia nodded. "Maybe you're right, Tim. But what else can we do to try to understand medical error?"

"I don't know," said Tim as he put his key in the ignition. "But it's weird how we can get it so right sometimes, and so wrong on other times. Maybe we should start looking at the times it goes really well, and try to learn from those episodes." Tim paused before he prepared to drive off. "I mean, have you seen what they do in Mr Thom's theatre for the checklist? It's amazing. I anaesthetise for him sometimes, and I've seen what they do. They've got the checklist down to a tee."

"No, I've not been in that theatre. I'll check it out. Thanks Tim."

Julia couldn't stop thinking about Tim's idea as she drove home. Why don't we investigate the episodes which go really well? Episodes of excellent practice are likely to have important learning points too, and would be a considerably more positive experience than a SIRI meeting. Julia felt a rising sense of optimism – by the time she got home she had made a pledge to herself to organise a 'reverse SIRI': an investigation into an episode of excellence. And she knew just the place to start...

"Welcome everyone. Thank you for coming to this reverse SIRI meeting. Before we start, shall we just do a quick round of introductions?" When she pitched the idea at a governance meeting, she had expected a lack of engagement for her cynical colleagues. Now she was pleasantly surprised at the response. She had asked Tim to 'report' the excellent practice in Mr Thom's theatre, and invited some of the theatre staff to attend the meeting, along with Tim and Sandra from the previous investigation. Tim started the introductions – Julia had been worried about him since the last SIRI. Like many colleagues, he was taking a long time to bounce back, and often appeared nervous or angry at work over the last few weeks. Today it looked like he had regained some of his spark.

As he introduced himself and explained that he had come up with the idea for investigating excellence, he seemed genuinely upbeat. James still came across as sensitive and positive, although he did have a slightly bemused look on his face. Sandra went next, appearing somewhat disinterested and the last two introductions were from members of the theatre team under investigation: a theatre nurse called Satnam who beamed from ear to ear throughout the whole meeting, and Robbie, an Operating Department Practitioner (ODP), who made a point of thanking Julia for the 'appreciation' of the work they do in Mr Thom's theatre. Mr Thom himself wasn't available, as he was giving a lecture on quality improvement at a major conference overseas.

"You're probably wondering how this meeting will work," said Julia, "as we haven't done this sort of thing before. It's an experiment really, so bear with me. I've done some serious thinking and I've come to the conclusion that we are missing learning opportunities from excellent practice. We tend to focus all our safety and quality improvement work on identifying and eliminating error. That's fine to a point, but I think we have ended up creating a culture of negativity. So when Tim told me about the way that the safety checklist is carried out in Mr Thom's theatre, I thought we should try to figure out what is going on there and see if it is possible to replicate it."

"Isn't this just 'sharing best practice'?" said Sandra.

"Well, yes," said Julia. "But that's not something that happens much around here. Can you remember the last time we did it?"

Sandra shrugged, as Julia carried on. "I initially thought we could try a root cause analysis approach, but on reflection, I don't think that methodology is adequate for our requirements. So I've done some reading and I came across a methodology called 'appreciative inquiry', or 'AI'. I want to give it a go, so bear with me."

"Sounds very funky," said Sandra in the most cynical tone in her repertoire.

The meeting then started with a description of what actually happens in Mr Thom's theatre during the checklist. Julia asked Tim, Satnam and Robbie to describe the whole process in as much detail as possible. Julia only spoke to seek clarification or to prompt for more detail. As the story unfolded, Julia became more certain that she was doing a good thing. The panel heard about proper teamwork. Each member of the theatre team, including Mr Thom, participated in the checklist; they took it in turns to lead the checklist, and everyone knew when it was their turn as the rota was written on the theatre wall. There was no hierarchy to speak of, and clearly a sense of cross-disciplinary respect. All theatre team members were on first name terms; Mr Thom was called Ulrich, apparently, which was news to Julia.

The panel learned that the theatre was silent during the checklists, except for the team members who were talking. Everyone gave it their full attention. The story went on and on, with a detailed description of a beautifully engaged team who prioritise safety. Tim, Satnam and Robbie gave several anecdotes to add weight to the whole story. Robbie explained that there is a prize for anyone who finds an error or problem which needs to be addressed – Robbie won the prize one day when he highlighted a patient's allergy to an antibiotic which would normally have been used in the surgical case. The 'prize' itself wasn't anything material, but simply a note of commendation and 'appreciation' written by Mr Thom and emailed directly to Robbie. Robbie described how he had used this as evidence in his recent appraisal.

As she looked around the room, Julia noticed that everyone was engaged, and Sandra had not checked her phone for at least ten minutes. She even noticed her taking some notes at one point.

As the meeting progressed, Julia steered the panel through other questions. She asked how they felt when they were working in this environment. "How does this line of enquiry help us?" Before Julia could continue, Satnam said, "It motivates me to do a good job. I feel like I'm valued and part of a team. It feels safe – for the patient and the staff." Sandra raised an eyebrow, then smiled and said "It feels safe? OK. I get that. Very interesting." She had lost her cynical tone.

Julia introduced the next topic for discussion, asking the panel to think about how to recreate this excellence in other theatres. After a short pause, Sandra spoke first. "It seems to me that you've got a really good thing going. I'd like to come and see it myself. Do you think I could come and observe?"

Satnam nodded. "Yes, of course. We could easily accommodate some observers if anyone would like to come and see for themselves."

"Like a showcase," said James.

"Yes, this is good," said Julia. "We could try to role-model this excellence."

"Perhaps we could write this up in some sort of report. And share it with everyone in the department. Like an excellence bulletin?" offered James.

"By highlighting excellence in the department, others might be able to emulate it," thought Julia. She looked up from her notes and saw that everyone was smiling and nodding. What a difference from the usual SIRI investigation.

The panel discussed other ideas to improve checklist behaviour, based on Mr Thom's theatre's practice. Some ideas were good; some were less good, but after a short while they produced a list of 'recommendations' and agreed to share these as learning points and suggestions for other theatres to adopt or learn from.

Just as Julia was about to call the meeting to a close, Tim spoke. "Julia, thanks for arranging this. It's been really great, and I think we should do more of it. It's clear that we can learn from excellence if we can develop a method to capture it. So how about a simple reporting system? To complement our adverse event reports, why don't we introduce a system for reporting excellence? Just a simple online form to capture some basic information; we could use it whenever we notice something excellent. It could be a great way to identify areas of good practice which warrant further investigation."

Sandra looked impressed. "Now that is a safety process I could really get on board with. It could be the antidote to adverse incident reporting." she said. "Shall we call it 'Learning from Excellence'?"

## About the author

*Adrian Plunkett is a consultant in Paediatric Intensive Care Medicine at Birmingham Children's Hospital. He has several clinical and non-clinical interests, but a common theme in all his work is a desire to discover new solutions to existing problems.*

# About Learning from Excellence

Traditionally, safety in healthcare has focused on avoiding harm by learning from error, but this approach may miss opportunities to learn from excellent practice. Excellence in healthcare is highly prevalent, but until recently there has been no formal system to capture it. In April 2014, a team at Birmingham Children's Hospital NHS Foundation Trust introduced *Learning from Excellence (LfE)*, which enables examples of excellent practice to be captured for individual and organisational learning. This programme uses AI to investigate the episodes of excellence. It also studies the impact of introducing LfE within teams and departments in the region through research projects and quality improvement interventions.

Since August 2016, Appreciating People (AP) has been working with the West Midlands Patient Safety Collaborative to deliver two-day "Taste of AI" training courses to support this Learning from Excellence approach and the introduction of AI more generally in healthcare. All five "Taste of AI" courses were fully booked and 15 more were then delivered. The participants were really interested in using AI to take another approach to learning and enhancing safety. They have responded by using AI to create positive education, and work on their quality improvement. It helped them build resilience, as they were focusing on the things they were good at, and celebrating their successes. This resulted in an Advanced AI Practitioner course to cultivate a community of experienced AI practitioners within the region who could share their experience more widely and an LfE Community Event for over 350 people to share knowledge and experience of the LfE approach and to discover new applications of these initiatives.

*Learning from Excellence* is an award-winning programme having won the 2017 Education and Training Award at the HSJ Patient Safety Awards. The judges felt that LfE "is a truly innovative approach that has the ability to transform the way we improve patient safety. This should be considered for national rollout both from patient safety and staff morale."

The LfE project is a demonstration of how AI can support a learning organisation. The tendency in many institutions – and indeed individually – is to focus on things that have gone wrong; to review what happened and to incorporate the learning into processes so that it doesn't happen again. The frequent effect of these review processes is to absorb considerable amounts of energy and time, within an atmosphere that someone or something was to blame and did 'something wrong'. It's difficult for people to learn in such an atmosphere.

Staff at Birmingham Children's Hospital are now encouraged to submit a simple LfE report whenever they see a team or a colleague doing something that they consider to be 'excellent'. These reports are collated and compiled into a newsletter to be shared around the organisation. Every few months, the LfE team selects a few of the excellent reports which they think offer good potential to learn from and they use an AI process to structure this learning. See **learningfromexcellence.com** and an Appreciating People website case study **www.appreciatingpeople.co.uk/portfolio/learning-from-excellence-quality-improvement**.

Whenever Adrian and his colleagues share their experience there is interest from staff in other organisations in UK and abroad, many of whom decide to develop their own version. The Patient Safety Collaborative of the West Midland Academic Health Science Network is dedicated to promoting and sharing good practice, so have supported the dissemination of the idea across the region. Since 2016, Appreciating People has been asked to provide AI training for staff within those organisations. During this training, staff see for themselves a range of other ways in which they could use AI internally and personally. The approach has been picked up by other areas including The Royal Hospital for Children, Glasgow, Liverpool Studio School and North West Ambulance Service.

The massive interest from NHS professionals across the UK indicates this work is making a great contribution to how they see learning and team-working. There are two strands worthy of research and further study. Firstly, the possibility that identifying performance at a deeper and more personal level, and identifying the learning opportunities at the earliest moment, means that *Learning from Excellence* takes discovering peak performance to a higher level.

The second strand is its importance in providing a practical and successful AI intervention that can challenge the more traditional way of learning by mistakes and errors. When things go wrong people are often feeling tense and defensive, so genuine and generative learning is more unlikely. There is a significant amount of research which indicates that optimum learning happens when people feel relaxed and positive – when things go right – then this learning can be applied as a way to reduce errors and support quality work.

# Part four: Tools, techniques and exercises – Reflecting on and deepening your AI practice

Here are some activities and suggestions to support your AI reflective process and how to get started with simple and practical AI interventions. Content includes activities to help understanding of the AI principles; how to start a simple AI intervention; a AI reflective practice tool, advice on AI protocol questions; a suggestion on generativity; how to hold a different kind of meeting; dealing with negativity; a suggestion on using the 5D cycle, the importance of intentions and plans, SOAR™ examples; an exercise on reframing, and information on Appreciative Living.

Our next Appreciating People publication, *Where did it all go so right?* (to be published in 2018), will contain practical resources and examples of AI in action for the more experienced AI practitioner.

# 1. Understanding and noticing the principles

Here are a couple of activities to help you understand the AI principles, how they interact and the contribution they can make to your AI practice. When you are at the beginning of your AI journey it is often difficult to fully understand them and their importance. Like anything, it takes practice. These activities will help you notice the AI principles at work and expand your understanding.

**i. Illustrating the principles with a film clip -** *Mr Holland's Opus*

If you don't know this film, add it to your list of useful AI films. The film stars Richard Dreyfuss in the title role of Glenn Holland, as a high-school music teacher who helps pupils on their musical journey and fosters the concept of musical excellence within an American high school, inspiring numerous students.

Go to YouTube and type in *Mr Holland's Opus – the clarinet scene*. Watch the clip and then consider these questions, either by yourself, or with other AI practitioners:

· Which principles were dominant and obvious?

· What was the impact of the AI principles?

· What did you notice about the AI principles at play?

· How did the exercise help you understand the AI principle?

· If working with a group you can repeat the viewing and the exercise noticing how the interplay of AI principles can change.

## ii. Observing AI principles in action

At the end of any AI intervention or project, use this AI protocol to reflect on the AI principles at work.

1. How has this AI intervention helped deepen your understanding of the AI principles?

2. What were the most obvious AI principles at work?

3. Which ones were subtly at work and why?

4. Reflecting on the AI principles at play what was the most unexpected thing you observed?

5. Which ones had the most impact? Provide an example of the impact.

6. How did the AI principles interact?

Read the AI principles card in *Taste of AI 2.0* and the 'further AI principles information sheet' found in AI resources on **www.appreciatingpeople.co.uk.**


## iii. Look at how the SIRI fable works (page 63) and what principles it is demonstrating

# 2. Starting with a simple intervention

You've completed an AI training workshop or you've read a lot around the subject and are itching to get started. Before you go into a full AI protocol or 5D cycle, start by dropping in a couple of different questions with colleagues or in a team meeting. Notice what is happening. Look at *A different kind of meeting* on page 87.

When you've experimented with a few conversations in different situations, use this mini protocol to reflect on your own learning. Either answer them yourself or ask a colleague to interview you.

· What was the reaction when you asked the questions?

· What did you learn and enjoy from the experience?

· What AI principles did you notice at play?

· What was different?

· What did you notice in yourself?

## Suggestion

*If a colleague is interviewing you, ask them to feed back any reactions they notice in you as you answer the questions.*

# 3. Simple reflective practice tool

A simple way to reflect on your growing AI practice is to ask yourself the following questions at the end of an AI intervention:

1. What worked really well and made a difference?

2. What was your best and most effective intervention?

3. What did you notice?

4. What was the hardest challenge and how did you meet it?

5. What were the most dominant principles at play?

6. What was your role and how did it help?

7. What did you learn and value?

8. What would you change next time?

9. Was there a point you engaged with the unknown/unexpected? How did it feel?

**Suggestion**

*You don't have to use all the questions – just those that are of most value to you.*

# 4. Being an Appreciative Inquirer – useful AI conversation questions

One of the best ways to help build your AI practice is to have useful questions for a variety of situations in your back pocket or notepad:

1. What would be the best thing to do now?
2. Given no constraints, what would you do?
3. What is great about what you do?
4. So what will you do that will work?
5. What is the best question I could ask?
6. What do we need to do differently?
7. What is the smallest thing, and/or the most radical thing, that you can do?
8. Would make a difference?
9. Isn't that interesting? Tell me more…
10. What are your top five strengths?
11. What do you value about what you do?
12. How do you know you will be successful?
13. How do we successfully deal with challenges?

Here are three questions which could be adapted to start a team meeting or awayday?

1. Tell me about a piece of work that you initiated or were involved in that went well.
2. What were the key elements that made it a good/inspiring/successful piece of work?
3 . Is there a way that you could bring any of the learning from this session into your time at work?

**Suggestion**

*In Appreciating People's experience, a useful question is 'what needs to be done differently?' It often tells us what's not working and the issues that need to be addressed – but avoiding a way that can easily spiral into negativity. You can also collect questions and protocols that help people from a negative standpoint. More information on coping with negativity is available on page 88.*

# 5. Planning a bigger AI intervention

You've completed a number of positive AI experiences, used AI questions in a meeting, designed and delivered a few mini-protocols. It's now time to try something a bit bigger – an AI activity using the 5D process or a SOAR™. Here are some practical suggestions to help you plan:

Create a table like the one below.

| Questions and tasks | Evidence and notes to self |
|---|---|
| What is the inquiry to be addressed? Have you got a topic? | |
| How was the inquiry topic identified and developed? How much of the 'system' was involved? | |
| What will success look like? | |
| What are the challenges that need to be addressed? | |
| Does the intervention require a project group? How were they selected and who do they represent? Does it reflect the whole system? | |
| If you are using either the 5D process or SOAR™ what are the steps you will take to complete the stages | |
| How will you design and test the protocols? | |
| How are you ensuring all the voices are heard? | |
| Have you got the right environment to work in? | |
| What equipment do you need to support you and how will you check it's all there and operational? | |
| Do you need people to help you, have you got them, and do they know their role? | |
| How are you going to introduce AI to people? Either to a planning, a wider group, or an organisation? | |
| Have you prepared your script for the process? | |
| What are your plans to evaluate the intervention? | |
| How will you identify the learning? | |
| What are your plans to follow up post intervention and to celebrate the impact and success? | |

On many occasions you don't need to mention you're using AI. It depends on the audience. Sometimes you may be responding to a specific request, on other occasions use language like 'we'll be working from people's strengths and assets, and identifying and building on what works and our achievements.'

## Suggestion

*While the majority of people will really enjoy and value the approach, some will struggle with AI. Sometimes it's outside their comfort zone, or they sense a perceived loss of power, fear of change or the challenge of unpicking years of thinking in a different way. Find a way to hear these views rather than ignore them, as they can make an important contribution.*

*What's important is to look for the generative and to observe the creative flow. Track and fan the things that you've done well; be aware of your own tendency to concentrate on negative responses rather than the encouraging and positive ones – we all have that tendency to dwell on perceived error, our negativity bias and reducing this in ourselves is part of our learning journey.*

# 6. The 5D cycle

Here, rather than outlining the 5D process, we have offered suggestions for consideration at each stage. Generally, the 5D cycle and AI summits are covered in initial AI training. We also want to highlight that – although people may think AI is just the 5D cycle and/or an AI summit – the reality is that it is much more than that. You can see how the 5D cycle fits together on page 49.

## Definition

- Remember the initial definition proposal may not be the real task. Be open to change and redefinition.
- Try and ensure there is buy-in at the highest level.
- It's all about positive phrasing – language that will engage and excite people.
- Try and engage people from across the system from the start, to get maximum support.
- Be prepared for outcomes to change as you go along – encourage flexibility and adaptability.

## Discovery

- Don't rush to the next stage – allocate plenty of time.
- Emphasise the importance of sharing stories and experiences.
- Remember that children and some cultures may struggle with paired conversations. You can use a group conversation with each person answering the question in turn – a talking stick is great for this.
- Take time to explain the process, the questions and feedback arrangements, including how the information will be used in the next stages.
- Encourage people to listen and foster dialogue.

## Dream

- As the dreams are based on the definition and discovery phases, they are based on reality and shared history. Encourage people to use all the data collected and shared in the discovery phase.
- When people present their dreams encourage the use of phrases such as 'we did this', 'we overcame the challenges by…'
- Some people might struggle with the term 'dream'. A useful introduction to this stage is to remind people that Martin Luther King had a dream – not a strategic plan.
- If children are present they often struggle with the dream stage, as thinking years ahead can be a challenge. Use the idea of being in Dr. Who's TARDIS or waking up from a long sleep, such as the Rip Van Winkle story.
- Encourage people to present back their dreams in a variety of ways. This

activity can be fun – don't be surprised when you get poetry, drama and wonderful visual images. Support people to move away from the flip-chart presentation. Be patient – it may take time and a bit of encouragement to get people going. You will be surprised what will emerge – it is often very moving as well as fun.

## Design

- Remember this is about designing the process and social architecture, not about doing it. A useful way to describe this stage is 'building the scaffolding'.
- Use intentions (page 81) instead of provocative propositions.
- Utilise the ideas from manufacturing and product design and 'prototype'. A 'product' may go through a number of prototypes, often failing at the first stage and requiring a rethink. That's how the best products emerge and are successful.
- Encourage small groups with defined actions and timescales and use conversations (protocols) to support the process.
- Remember that AI differs from other vision and forward thinking methodologies. It supports further working arrangements which are grounded in existing strengths, success and skills. It fosters improvisation and adaptability. This stage can be hard work – it can and will challenge historic practice and embedded cultures and may meet resistance.

## Destiny/Delivery

- One of the dictionary definitions of destiny is 'the predetermined or inevitable course of events'.
- The purpose of this stage is to sustain momentum so groups, individuals and organisations can build capacity to do the work. It builds on the positive energy, creativity and co-design developed in the early stages. This is often called 'maintaining an appreciative eye'.
- AI evidence suggests that momentum for change and long-term sustainability increase when conventional implementation arrangements like formal action planning and monitoring progress are used sparingly. Encourage innovation and foster learning and reflection.
- Say '**yes to the mess**' and accept that transformation requires improvisation, adaptability and flexibility.
- Remember the 5D process is not just circular – you can do mini-cycles at each stage.

## Suggestion:

*In the Nepal village banks they have two extra Ds – **Do it** and **Dance and Drum** – a useful reminder to always celebrate success!*

# 7. Intentions and different leadership approach – an alternative to plans

**Do you have an intention for your organisation, or do you have a plan?**

Perhaps you have neither, of course. The only challenge with neither is that it's very easy to get distracted with tempting opportunities that may lead you to never complete anything, not follow up with someone, or end up wandering around with no sense of accomplishment or purpose.

Not that that's bad, but it may be somewhat dissatisfying. The concept of 'intentions' and their use in leadership and the 5D cycle, is an interesting alternative to more traditional views on leadership and planning such as mission statements, aims and objectives and five-year plans.

David Marquet's work on intent-based leadership is helpful here: "Leadership should mean giving control rather than taking control, and creating leaders rather than forging followers. Communities are built by volunteers who choose to do their work for free. The rules for building a community are the opposite of those in old-fashioned organisations. Instead of telling people what to do spend time talking about intent."

*Turn The Ship Around!: A True Story of Building Leaders by Breaking the Rules* (2013)

It's not about having a plan and sticking to it – it's about having an intention. A successful leader recognises the chaos, incomplete information, changes in situation, and other factors that may make a plan obsolete when executed. The role of a successful leader is to empower others and guide their initiative and improvisation as they adapt a plan to a changing environment.

Such a leader is vital in chaotic, demanding, and dynamic environments. A traditional planning approach with aims and objectives with a fixed timescale can be quickly out of date and limiting. However, an intention allows for flexibility, clarity of purpose and simplicity. Keep intentions simple, clear and flexible. If you can say it one sentence all the better – it can always be expanded upon.

Remember Eisenhower's quote: 'Plans are nothing, planning is everything'. How many organisations' plans are unrealistically detailed and formulaic? Or are not relevant to the changing realities and sit in drawers gathering dust? They may have been made by the few and not involved all the voices. The intention approach provides a planning framework that fits well with an AI approach of co-designing and co-creating at the design and destiny stages. It is flexible and adaptable and can include detailed plans when required which clearly meet the intention.

## Suggestion

- Any action or plan that does not meet the intention is not undertaken
- Review intentions periodically to check if they are still relevant
- Create action plans that have short delivery timescales that are achievable

# 8. A different form of action plan

Here is a slightly different, more user-friendly approach to creating action plans. For some people, action plans are helpful, whilst for others it's a turn-off. The titles can be changed – you could try 'No money, Some money and Abundance'.

Use a large flip chart for the model and write down the actions on Post-it notes so that they can be easily moved around and grouped. Then use 'design to delivery' groups to help deliver the actions. Remember to feed back and communicate achievements and progress to help sustain engagement and continued commitment.

## Activity

| Now | Sooner | Later |
|-----|--------|-------|
|     |        |       |

# 9. Noticing generativity

*"AI can be generative in a number of ways. It is the quest for new ideas, images, theories and models that liberate our collective aspirations, alter the social construction of reality and, in the process, make available decisions and actions that were not available or did not occur to us before. When successful, AI generates spontaneous, unsupervised, individual, group and organisational action toward a better future."* Gervase Bushe

Fostering and encouraging generativity is a key component to Appreciative Inquiry. When it's present, AI will make a long-lasting difference. Essentially, it means generating new (and actionable) ideas. All AI should be generative – it's an idea that underpins AI practice, as its unique, appreciative style is designed to energise and inspire, by challenging assumptions, encouraging deep dialogue and exploring fundamental questions.

Look for the way people lean into each other during paired conversations and actively listen. You'll notice the levels of purposeful noise, laughter; the creativity and cooperation of people, release of energy and the quality of the emergent actions.

**Suggestion**

*Following an AI facilitated session, reflect on these questions:*

1. *How did generativity appear?*

2. *What was its impact?*

3. *What did you learn about it?*

# 10. Reframing

Reframing is an important process in both designing and delivering appreciative conversations. Responses are always very different when using this exercise, and sharing ideas is a major part of the learning.

Positive psychology studies of the brain show that focusing on problems triggers our brain's fear responses, lowering our ability to find solutions. Positive emotions (joy, contentment) broaden our thought–action repertoire, expanding the range of behaviours. (Have a look at the Positive Principle on page 56.) These broadened mindsets build an individual's resources. So it pays to observe unhelpful, limiting thoughts and replace them with more positive thoughts and perspectives.

A picture can look very different according to the frame it is put in. Reframing allows us to take any situation or experience and view it through a different lens – or place it in an alternative 'frame'. Deliberate and conscious positive reframing draws on the AI principles and allows us to view our experience in a new light. It is a powerful way to transform our thinking and supports resilience and creativity. Are you broadening and building or narrowing your response options?

An easy way to practice reframing is by noticing the language that we use and soften it, for instance – 'I don't have enough qualifications' can be reframed to 'how can I improve my learning and qualifications?'

Ask about the underlying enthusiasm or wish, and explore what might be unexpressed. For example, consider 'what might we want more of?' or 'how might we have succeeded in the past?' If someone says 'team meetings are boring' then you can reframe by asking 'what would make meetings interesting?'

# Reframing in practice

Reframing involves noticing how we see something and choosing to see it differently, just as a picture can be transformed by changing the frame that it's in. It plays a key role in appreciative conversations and elsewhere in Appreciative Inquiry methods.

Individually or in small groups, consider the issues and matters in the left hand column. Reframe and compose possible options in the right hand column. The first one provides an example. There will be a number of options. Choose the issues which are most relevant to your situation at the present time. When you've found a reframe that you like, design some appreciative questions to help you explore that affirmative topic.

At the end, reflect on the experience of reframing each issue – share possible answers in the large group. Remember that there are multiple ways of reframing and each can provide a useful basis for discussion.

| Issues and concerns | Reframe, first as a 'topic' (there could be a number of alternatives), then design a linked appreciative question... |
|---|---|
| Poor leadership | *Great leadership* <br> *Q. Tell me about some examples of good leadership you have seen or read about?* <br> *Q. What strengths do good leaders have?* <br> *Q. What do you value in good leadership?* |
| Staff don't feel listened to | |
| Poor teamwork | |
| Low staff morale | |
| Poor staff engagement | |
| Inadequate training | |
| Lack of safety | |

# 11. Appreciative Living

The book *Appreciative Living* and the associated development work by Jackie Kelm was an Appreciative Inquiry game changer. It demonstrated how AI could be used by individuals and groups, and contributed to it being used more widely than the more common large-scale OD interventions. *Appreciative Living* offers many ways of 'building the appreciative muscle'. This person-centred use of *Appreciative Living* is about embedding the principles of Appreciative Inquiry into everyday work and life. It is a mindset – as well as a set of tools for living and working in an appreciative, strengths-based, generative way, that leads to outstanding performance, high engagement, and exceptional results.

*Appreciative Living* helps people see hidden possibilities, strengths, and opportunities for improvement, innovative solutions, and the generative potential in any situation. It is learning how to discover and bring out the best in ourselves and each other to unleash our human potential, creative genius, and innate collaborative spirit that often lies dormant in more traditional problem-focused ways of knowing and being. It is about tapping into our highest aspirations individually and collectively to get clear about what we want most, and find the strength and inspiration within to make our greatest dreams come to life.

*Appreciative Living* has been used to help people overcome depression, to find joy in living with serious conditions such as Multiple Sclerosis, and overcome devastating loss and grief. It has also been used to help people create extraordinary lives, find meaning and joy in their work again, and transform difficult relationships. It is a universal set of tools and approaches that can transform our everyday work and lives to create greater success and happiness.

To learn more about *Appreciative Living*, visit **www.AppreciativeLiving.com**, where you'll find articles, workshops, books, and more. There is also a free mini-book on getting started, which includes simple exercises you can do right away to see immediate results.

# 12. Facilitating a different kind of meeting

For many people, the traditional committee or meeting rituals can be a turn-off. Here are some suggestions for alternative approaches based on practical experience.

a) Consider changing the agenda so that minutes and matters arising are placed in the middle or at the end of the meeting. Discuss and agree the most important items and do them first. This will always give more time to the essential business and can help animate participants.

b) Start your meetings with simple exercises such as asking each participant to answer some of these questions:
'What would be the best thing to come out of this meeting?'
'What, for you, would make this meeting a success?' 'Since our last meeting what have we achieved? It can be a small thing.'
'What is the most important thing we need to address?'

c) During the meeting, suggest exploring agenda items by breaking into pairs with a question on one of the topics, and then feeding back. If the group is large, move the pairs into sixes after the paired conversation and then do group feedback.

d) End the meeting with simple exercises, such as:

   · Ask each participant to write down on a Post-it note the one action they will do to help deliver the agreed actions.

   · Ask questions like 'what has been the most important thing we have achieved to today?' 'Have we met your meeting intentions that you raised at the beginning?' 'What have we enjoyed and found valuable?'

These ideas foster better engagement, wider conversations, support creativity and make meetings more enjoyable.

(This activity has been taken from *Appreciating Church* (2017) – available from **www.aiessentials.co.uk**.)

# 13. Ways of dealing with problems, challenges, issues and negativity

One of the great challenges is handling negativity and people's traditional focus and concentration on issues and problem solving. From our AI experience, we still notice our own tendency to focus on a negative comment, even though it might be surrounded by a sea of positive ones!

A key learning point in any AI journey is the move away from identifying problems and away from the wish for a quick resolution. The suggestions below are drawn from *Appreciative Inquiry, Change at the speed of imagination.* (Magruder Watkins, Mohr and Kelly)

· Traditional problem solving looks for what is wrong and 'fixes' it – thereby returning the situation to the status quo.
· AI solves problems by seeking what is going right and building on it, going beyond the original 'normal baseline' of correcting the error. It allows the possibility of something new to be included, which makes the service/activity better.

Having embraced the concept of the socially constructed reality, we can look at problems from the AI perspective based on these assumptions:
· 'The way things are' is socially constructed by our system and therefore can be changed;
· In any situation, we can find the seeds of excellence to build on;
· We build on excellence by seeking out examples and sharing stories throughout the system;
· As we create images of excellence, our system will move toward that image.

The process of solving 'problems' in the emerging paradigm follows:
· Let's look at our experience in the area that we want to improve. When were things going well? When did we feel excited, successful and joyful?
· From these stories we can collectively create a description for what we're seeking (our image of the ideal).
· Ask others how they have successfully dealt with a similar situation.
· Share our images; discover the images that others hold and continually re-create a generative and creative future throughout the system.

Moving from the problem solving approach takes time and practice. The Centre of Learning from Excellence in Birmingham has drawn from

Cooperrider to develop user-friendly suggestions for 'Reporting on Excellence'. It includes a good summary of advice for facilitators and interviewers on dealing with the negatives. (Page 70 for information on the LfE project.) The aim of this process is learning from positives, but people should feel like they also have permission to also talk about things that need fixing. There are several different ways to handle negatives.

1. **Postponing**: Say that you would like to make a note of what the person has said and come back to it later. When you get to the question about what he or she would wish for the organisation in the future, this is the time to discuss the 'negative' data.

2. **Listening**: If the person has some real intensity about problems, let them express it. If it is the major focus of the person's energy, you are not going to get anything positive until she or he gets it out. This may mean muddling through quite a bit of organisational negativity, and the biggest threat is that you will take it in and lose your capacity to be appreciative. Keep a caring, and affirmative spirit.

3. **Redirecting**: If the person is adamant about dealing with the negative, or if you have listened sufficiently to understand the negative issues being raised, find a way to guide the person back to the positive: "I think I understand a little bit about some of the problems you see (paraphrase a few of the ones you've heard), and now I would like to guide us back to looking at what is happening when things are working at their best.

4. **Using negative data to find a positive reframe**: Everything that people find wrong with an organisation represents an absence of something that they hold in their minds as an ideal. For example, if the interviewee says something like, "The communication in this organisation is terrible"; say to them, "When you say that the communication is terrible, it means that you have some image in your mind about what good communication would look like. Can you describe that for me?" In fact, one could argue that there is no such thing as negative data – use negative information and reframe it into a wish or vision statement and then confirm that statement with the interviewee.

5. **Don't get worried when you come across negativity** – it's how humans are wired and it takes time to rewire. For some people it is just too difficult and not for them. Retain a benevolent curiosity as much as possible. Reframing is really helpful here (page 84). Don't close it down – take a different approach to letting it be heard but not dominating discussions and energy, such as using the *Issues Wall*, which is covered in the following activity.

# 14. The Issues Wall, or 'Park it!'

Another useful tool for tackling negativity is the Issues Wall or 'Park it!' exercise. At the beginning of an event/workshop, place flip-chart paper on a wall or stand and mark it either Issues/ Challenges Wall, or 'Park it!'

Invite participants to write on a Post-it note any issues, problems or challenges they think need to be addressed or voiced. When they've written their comments, ask them to place them on the flip-chart. Let them know that they can add to them at any time, promising that at the end of the workshop these concerns will be revisited. Experience shows a number of things often happen:

· Recording and writing matters down is often sufficient for people. They just want their concerns raised and noticed.

· For the facilitator, it can help you gauge the concern level. You can often reframe and weave them into the process. Sometimes, if you have time, it's useful to cluster comments together into common themes.

· Often, there's a correlation between the matters raised and the answers to the question 'what needs to be done differently?'

· Don't forget to revisit the wall at the end of the workshop. You'll often find that participants say 'it's been covered' or 'we've dealt with it in a different way...'

· Occasionally, when there important issues that still need to be addressed, depending on circumstances, you might need to feed back the concerns and issues to the wider organisation/management. This is a facilitator judgment call.

# 15. SOAR™ (Strengths, Opportunities, Aspirations, Results/Resources)

*"The task of leadership is to create an alignment of strengths, making our weaknesses irrelevant."* Peter Drucker

SOAR™ is the Appreciative Inquiry contribution to strategic planning, and a generative alternative to a SWOT analysis. Moving from the dominant threats and weaknesses elements of SWOT, the SOAR™ approach encourages a more innovative and positive approach to strategic planning.

It was created and trademarked by Jackie Stavros and Gina Hinrichs (see: *The Thin Book of SOAR™: building strengths-based strategy, 2009*). Focusing on strengths and opportunities for individuals and organisations is much more powerful and effective than dwelling on deficiencies. SOAR™ helps to generate enthusiasm and create positive momentum. Weaknesses and threats are not ignored; they are reframed and given the appropriate focus within the opportunities and results conversations.

As it is with AI, SOAR™ is a circular process – the process of identifying strengths, opportunities, and aspirations, can lead to the discovery of additional opportunities.

Traditionally, the SOAR™ tool has been used in the design element of the 5D process. However, increasingly, SOAR™ has been used as a standalone tool and in large scale interventions. We've supplied three examples.

**Suggestion**

You can design a SOAR™ for nearly any situation. The examples provided can be adapted and changed to meet local circumstances. You don't have to use all the questions – they're a resource to pick from – develop and add your own.

If people are wedded to the need to explore weaknesses and threats then use SWOT as a first stage. When they get used to SOAR™ they will find SWOT usage diminishes. Depending on the context the 'R' can stand for either resources or results.

# A SOAR™ for the AI practitioner journey

This is a SOAR™ to use as an AI practitioner reflective and learning tool. We suggest it's completed twice a year and is used in Appreciating People's advanced AI programme.

| Strengths | Opportunities |
|---|---|
| What are the best parts of your current AI activities?<br><br>What do you enjoy about your AI practice?<br><br>When do you know you have been effective?<br><br>What are the skills and strengths you bring to your AI journey?<br><br>What do you value about your AI work?<br><br>What other experiences and skills can you blend into your AI practice? | What are the opportunities out there for your AI work to flourish?<br><br>Consider what opportunities can build your strengths and skills?<br><br>How can you maximise and utilise the opportunities out there?<br><br>What AI experiences do you wish to explore and learn more about? |
| **Aspirations** | **Resources/Results** |
| Why are you passionate about AI?<br><br>What do you want do more with your AI work?<br><br>It's two year's time and you are reflecting on your AI journey to this point. What is different and what have you achieved?<br><br>What do you need to do differently with you AI practice? | What resources do you need to meet your AI journey aspirations and opportunities?<br><br>What is the smallest action you need to do and the most innovative?<br><br>When will you know that you are confident AI practitioner?<br><br>How will you know your AI experience and knowledge will be different? |

# Personal development SOAR™

This SOAR™ has been adapted from the personal development SOAR™ created for *How to Be More Awesome* (available from **www.aiessentials.co.uk**).

| Strengths | Opportunities |
|---|---|
| What are your most powerful strengths?<br><br>What do your friends, colleagues or family members think you are good at?<br><br>What do you enjoy and value about what you do?<br><br>What are your core values? Give an example…<br><br>What special skills and knowledge do you have? (Something you would like to use more of…) | Create a list of the most important opportunities available out there<br><br>Consider what opportunities could use your skills and strengths more?<br><br>Who could you talk with to help you identify different possibilities?<br><br>What would be the most exciting and challenging opportunity you could consider? |
| **Aspirations** | **Results/Resources** |
| What are the aspirations you have already met?<br><br>What are you passionate about?<br><br>What excites you about life and/or work?<br><br>What do you want to achieve and do more of?<br><br>What would it look like if you had already achieved it? | Who could you help you to meet your aspirations?<br><br>What resources do you need to meet your aspirations and to maximise your opportunities?<br><br>What are the first two things you need to do?<br><br>How will you know you have achieved anything and how would you measure your success?<br><br>How could you celebrate your achievements? |

# A SOAR™ tool for small teams looking to explore and co-create their future

| Strengths | Opportunities |
|---|---|
| What does the team do well?<br><br>What are its successes when it is working at its best?<br><br>What are the top five strengths in the team?<br><br>What skills, knowledge and expertise could team members contribute more of?<br><br>What have been the major achievements? | What are the existing opportunities for this team to flourish?<br><br>What are the opportunities internally that can be utilised more?<br><br>Who – and in what ways – are the other people who could support this team?<br><br>What are the innovative opportunities that this team could work on? |
| **Aspirations** | **Results/Resources** |
| What is the passion and motivation of this team?<br><br>What does this team aspire to do more of?<br><br>What successes and changes might you see in the team in 12 months' time?<br><br>What new ways of working and providing services might you see in the organisation over the next 18 months? | What are the resources needed to move forward?<br><br>What are the first steps and smallest actions you can take?<br><br>What would be the most innovative?<br><br>How will you know you have got there?<br><br>What will it look like? |

| Strengths | Opportunities |
|---|---|
|  |  |
| **Aspirations** | **Resources/Results** |
|  |  |

| Strengths | Opportunities |
|---|---|
| | |
| **Aspirations** | **Resources/Results** |
| | |

| Strengths | Opportunities |
|-----------|---------------|
|           |               |
| **Aspirations** | **Resources/Results** |
|           |               |

# Notes

# Notes

# Part five: The *Reflections* Team

**Sponsors and contributors**

*Reflections* wouldn't have been developed without sponsorship from the WMAHSN, the David. L. Cooperrider Center for Appreciative Inquiry, Champlain College Vermont USA and Appreciating Church.

**WMPSC and WMAHSN**

The West Midlands Patient Safety Collaborative (WMPSC), hosted by the West Midlands Academic Health Science Network (WMAHSN), supports members with innovative solutions to help deliver on improving patient safety. It aims to improve safety and continually reduce avoidable harm by helping organisations to work together to develop, implement, share and spread proven safety practice and interventions based on rigorous, evidence-based scientific methodologies.

The WMPSC focuses on co-design and co-production with members and the spread of successful innovative approaches through a networked approach. The WMPSC continues to nurture and support a region-wide network focused on the improvement of patient safety across care settings, enabling sharing of best practice and innovation in patient safety.

The WMAHSN leads, catalyses and drives co-operation, collaboration and productivity between academia, industry, health and care providers and commissioners, and citizens, and accelerate the adoption of innovation to generate continuous improvement in the region's health and wealth. The West Midlands AHSN will maintain a shared purpose and shared endeavour across its members and partners; it will at all times be honest, transparent, inclusive and innovative. The purpose of WMAHSN is to deliver improved healthcare outcomes and create economic growth.

**David L. Cooperrider Center for Appreciative Inquiry Champlain College Vermont USA**

The David L. Cooperrider Center for Appreciative Inquiry is the global Center of Excellence in Appreciative Inquiry and strengths-based organisational management. Based in the Robert P. Stiller School of Business at Champlain College in Burlington, Vermont, the center provides cutting-edge educational offerings in AI and Positive Organisational Development, AI-related organisational consultancy services, and serves as a knowledge incubator that advances the theory and practice of AI across all organisational sectors around the world.
www.champlain.edu/appreciativeinquiry

Appreciating People provides AI training resources to the AI certification programme.

Taste of AI 2.0 is a wonderful pragmatic, yet generative tool for helping individuals and organisations learn not only what Appreciative Inquiry is, but how they can apply it in meaningful ways to create positive change. Our students at the Cooperrider Center for Appreciative Inquiry have found them to be an extremely useful resource for their learning and applied practice with others."

Dr. Lindsey Godwin, Director of the David L. Cooperrider Center for AI, Champlain College

**Appreciating Church**

Appreciating Church is an UK ecumenical project initiated and led by the United Reformed Church, in partnership with the Methodist Church, Quakers, and the Congregational

Federation, with interest from individual dioceses of the Church of England and others. This resource is part of a programme to create a self-sustaining AI community of practice across the Church. The programme aims to foster and encourage the church at a local and national level to engage people in an inclusive way, listening to 'all the voices', building on our existing strengths and skills, counting our blessings and co-creating a resilient church as part of the kingdom of Heaven.

As of August 2017, over 250 people have participated in AI training workshops and a number of AI-based events and projects have been delivered. In February 2017, Appreciating Church – in partnership with Appreciating People – launched the book *Appreciating Church*. A practical guide to AI theory and practice, it includes stories of how to use AI within churches. (See **www. appreciating.church**)

## Acknowledgements

Adrian and Emma Plunkett developed the original model for Learning from Excellence and have given tirelessly of their time in sharing experience about it and supporting people who want to develop their own version. Peter Jeffries and Helen Hunt, supported by many of their colleagues, have creatively and passionately gone beyond their WMAHSN duties to promote the spread of AI and LfE. We are delighted to be their partners in winning the MSJ award for education and training.

There are a number of people, who have given advice, helped in the thinking, made contributions, provided sponsorship and have been a test bed for some of the activities. These include many of the clients listed on the Appreciating People website. Special thanks go to Kieran Bohan, Helen Bush, Jeanie Cockell, Jim Coleman, Lindsey Godwin, Helen Hunt, Peter Jeffries, Joan McArthur Blair, Sue McGavin, Francesca Olivia, Mary Patrick, Cati Paya, Matthew Reed, Anita Sheehan, Robyn Stratton-Berkessel, Mike Taylor, Fiona Thomas, Joan Wilmot, Andrea McGuiness and Jane Walsh.

**Appreciating People** works with people, communities, business, charities and organisations to help them get the best out of themselves. Working regionally, nationally and internationally from its base in Liverpool, UK, Appreciative Inquiry lies at the heart of everything it does. Its work supports organisational development, resilience, adaptability, innovation and wellbeing across local authorities, private businesses, communities, hospitals, universities and social enterprises, see **www.appreciatingpeople.co.uk**.

Appreciating People is the principle AI training provider and coach for the *Appreciating Church* programme, trainer for the WMASHN Learning from Excellence programme, and partners with the David L Cooperrider at the Center for AI, Champlain College in Vermont, USA.

**AI essentials** is a range of AI resources written by Appreciating People and published by Wordscapes. For product details go to **www.aiessentials.co.uk**

### Cover illustrator: Wendy Richardson

Wendy trained as a fine artist, known for her vibrant paintings and portraits. In March 2017 her series of abstract paintings were exhibited at the Moray Arts Centre. When not working she enjoys walking her dog on the beach and eating ice cream with her children. You can contact Wendy via **hello@appreciatingpeople.co.uk**.

# Glossary of terms

A brief explanation of some the AI terms used in reflections

**5D cycle**
One of the core AI tools, the 5Ds cycle is used to design protocols, projects, AI summits, projects and programmes. The 4D cycle is also in common use (without the 'definition' stage).

**Appreciative conversation**
'Appreciative conversation' is an alternative to the traditional AI term – 'protocol' or 'interview'. It is generally used to encourage and emphasise informality and reflection.

**Appreciative Inquiry**
An organisational development approach and philosophy based on an organisation's or person's strengths. It engages people in studying and building on 'what works'. According to Bushe, 'AI revolutionised the field of organisation development and was a precursor to the rise of positive organisation studies and the strengths-based movement in American management.'

**AI principles**
These underpin the philosophy behind Appreciative Inquiry. There are five main ones – constructionist, simultaneity, anticipatory, poetic and positive. Other principles are emerging all the time, including the wholeness, enactment and awareness principles.

**AI protocol**
The term AI practitioners use to determine the sequence and focus of an appreciative conversation/interview. Protocols can vary in length from three to eight questions. They are normally a paired conversation, but can be a group conversation.

**AI summit**
A large group method for accelerating positive change in organisations and communities, involving a broad range of internal and external stakeholders. It is designed to discover an organisation or community's core competencies and strengths; envision opportunities for positive change; design desired changes in systems, structures, strategies and cultures, and implement and sustain the changes.

**Appreciative journaling**
Appreciative journaling focuses on recording and reflecting on positive, life affirming and generative experiences. The approach draws on Positive Psychology and the science of wellbeing.

**Appreciative living**
First coined by Jackie Kelm in her pioneering book *Appreciative Living*, it encourages the use of AI in personal and family situations and encourages developing the appreciative muscle and mindset.

**Appreciative mindset**
An appreciative mindset is where an AI practitioner's journey has reached the point where their AI knowledge, thinking and approach is embedded and comes easily to the fore in their work and life. They are increasingly skilled in reframing, indentifying the good, and recognising positive potential.

**Appreciative muscle**
In her book *Appreciative Living*, Jackie Kelm encourages readers to practice and build their 'appreciative muscle' – in the same way they would strengthen their physical ones.

## Broaden-and-build
Barbara Frederickson's theory explains how positive emotions broaden the scope of our attention and our thought-action repertoires, and build psychological resilience and improved emotional wellbeing.

## Generativity
Generativity is a key concept in AI, meaning generating new and actionable ideas. It underpins all AI practice and it is designed to energise and inspire.

## Intentions
An intention is a statement of a future position which an organisations or group aspires to achieve. Intentions – as opposed to detailed plans – encourage delegation, flexibility, creativity and adaptability. In AI, intentions can be used as an alternative to provocative propositions and future statements.

## Learning from Excellence
The idea of Learning from Excellence is about shifting to a more positive culture of recognising and appreciating excellence in the workplace. The initiative allows staff members to 'report' excellence when they see it, provide formal positive feedback to one another, and identify parts of the system which are working well.

## Positive Psychology
Positive Psychology is the scientific study of the strengths that enable individuals and communities to thrive – to lead meaningful and fulfilling lives, to cultivate what is best within themselves, and to enhance their experiences of love, work, and play.

## Provocative propositions
Part of the 'design' stage in the 5D framework, the term 'provocative' is meant to challenge people and make them think. Propositions are uplifting statements about how a group goes forward, co-designs and co-creates its future – they are sometimes called 'future statements'.

## Reframing
Reframing involves consciously noticing how we see something and choosing to see it differently – just as a picture can be transformed by changing its frame. Its influence can be transformational in supporting creativity and different ways of thinking.

## SIRI
A Serious Incident Requiring Investigation is a process for reviewing mistakes and errors within UK National Health Service (NHS). Most institutions have their own process for investigating and learning from these incidents.

## SOAR™
SOAR™ is the Appreciative Inquiry alternative to the SWOT analysis, focusing on positives, rather than negatives. It was created by Jackie Stavros and Gina Hinrichs.

## Social constructionism
This theory describes how our world can be constructed by language and communication and by our thinking and our memories. It suggests that what we consider to be true – including basic everyday realities – is derived from our socialisation, social interactions, and our shared assumptions about reality. The concept of social construction predates AI (Berger and Luckman's *The Social Construction of Reality* was published in 1966).